D1362393

LANGUAGE-ARTS EXPLORER

POSTWAR
UNITED
STATES

1945 to the 1970s

by Maggie Combs

HISTORY DIGS

CHERRY LAKE PUBLISHING • ANN ARBOR, MICHIGAN

CHERRY LAKE Publishing

Published in the United States of America
by Cherry Lake Publishing
Ann Arbor, Michigan
www.cherrylakepublishing.com

Printed in the United States of America
Corporate Graphics Inc.
September 2011
CLFA09

Consultants: Michelle Kuhl, associate professor of history, University of Wisconsin Oshkosh;
Gail Saunders-Smith, associate professor of literacy, Beeghly College of Education,
Youngstown State University

Editorial direction: Design and production:
Rebecca Rowell   Marie Tupy

Photo credits: AP Images, cover, 1, 5, 17, 18, 25; Pamela Moore/iStockphoto, 6; George Marks/
Retrofile/Getty Images, 8; Shutterstock Images, 9, 21; Dan Grossi/AP Images, 11; HO/AP
Images, 13; Marty Lederhandler/AP Images, 15, 23, 30; Glenn R. McGloughlin/Shutterstock
Images, 27

Library of Congress Cataloging-in-Publication Data
Combs, Maggie, 1985-
 Postwar United States / by Maggie Combs.
    p. cm. – (Language arts explorer–History digs)
 ISBN 978-1-61080-196-6 – ISBN 978-1-61080-284-0 (pbk.)
 1. United States–Civilization–1945—Juvenile literature. 2. United States–History–1945—
Juvenile literature. 3. United States–Social conditions–1945—Juvenile literature. 4. United
States–Social life and customs–20th century–Juvenile literature. I. Title.
 E169.12.C578 2011
 973.91–dc22

                                    2011015121

**Cherry Lake Publishing would like to acknowledge the work of The Partnership for
21st Century Skills. Please visit www.21stCenturySkills.org for more information.**

TABLE OF CONTENTS

You are being given a mission. The facts in What You Know will help you accomplish it. Remember the clues from What You Know while you are reading the story. The clues and the story will help you answer the questions at the end of the book. Have fun on this adventure!

YOUR MISSION

Your mission is to learn to think like a historian. What tools do historians use to research the past? What kinds of questions do they ask, and where do they look for answers? On this assignment, your goal is to investigate the changes that happened in America after World War II (1939–1945) until the early 1970s. How did Americans react to the end of World War II? How did they view the Cold War and the Vietnam War that followed? What impact did those events have on daily life? Be sure to remember facts from What You Know as you read.

WHAT YOU KNOW

★ The end of World War II fueled Americans' desire to be financially secure and own a house—the so-called American dream. This led to increased spending and the growth of **suburbs**.

★ The Cold War was a time of tension between the Soviet Union and the United States. Each superpower was afraid of nuclear attack by the other. The United States tried to keep **communism** from spreading.

★ Jackie Robinson was the first African American to play major league baseball. He broke racial boundaries and lived his life for the civil rights cause. The civil rights movement fought against racial prejudice and for racial equality.

★ In the Vietnam War, the United States helped South Vietnam fight North Vietnam and its attempt to spread communism. It was a long conflict that the United States did not win.

The end of World War II was cause for celebration for Americans. It marked the beginning of an era of growth and prosperity for the United States.

★ Vietnam War protesters highlighted a **counterculture** known as the **hippie** movement. This culture was known for its music, promotion of peace and love, and drug use.

Use this book to explore history in ways a historian might. A student is exploring U.S. history during this time and keeping a journal of her discoveries. Carry out your mission by reading the student's journal.

It's summer break and I'm traveling with my mom. She's **curator** of the museum in our small town. She's preparing an **exhibit** on life in the United States after World War II. This didn't sound very fun to me, but I was excited when my mom said our first road trip would be to the Museum of Broadcast Communications in Chicago to explore the history of television.

We toured some exhibits before heading into the **archives** room. There was a lot to see, but my mom sat at a computer. She said the museum converted its television shows and commercials into digital files. Her goal was to find clips to help visitors to her exhibit understand what life was like for an American family in the 1950s.

The American Dream

As we watched commercials, I was surprised by how many of them focused on the kitchen. They advertised the newest appliances or a new food that would make cooking easier. We watched more than five refrigerator commercials. And we watched commercials for Spam and Bisquick that claimed the products would make a housewife's life easier. My mom explained that in the 1950s, families were moving out of the cities to pursue the American dream of owning a house. They also wanted the latest household inventions that made keeping that house easier for the mother of the family.

"People didn't own houses before the 1950s?" I asked her. She laughed a little.

"Some people did," she explained. "Life after the war was very different than before it.

6

The nation had widespread suffering during the Great Depression. Millions lost their jobs and couldn't afford basics such as food and housing. The war boosted industry. Supplies were needed for the troops. This economic growth continued after the war. Companies switched from making war goods to creating products consumers wanted, such as televisions and refrigerators. There was a boom in the economy and in babies, too. Young men returning from the war married and started families."

"So, the end of the war was good in two ways," I said. "The fighting stopped and the country was in better shape."

"That's right," Mom said. "There was a renewed hope in the future. In the 1950s, the suburbs formed as families sought to raise their children away from the cities. Many families were able to buy a house with the help of the government. It gave many veterans low-interest loans.

FIRST CREDIT CARD

The first credit card, called the Diners Club card, was created in 1950. A credit card allows a person to instantly borrow money to make purchases. The credit card user has to pay the money back later. The cards made spending easier and led to its increase. An average person's debt doubled during the 1950s. In the economic crisis of the early 2000s, Americans decreased their debt and relied less on credit cards. Debit cards, which deduct money directly from a bank account instead of borrowing it, became popular. They allow people to have easy access to their money without overspending.

A typical suburban house in the 1950s

"Those who moved to the suburbs expected the **domestic** bliss portrayed in commercials," she explained. "But they actually found houses placed closely together with very few upgrades. Sometimes, the houses looked identical. Wives were expected to stay home and care for the family and house. Husbands worked long hours to provide for their family's suburban life."

"Moms must have wanted to get out of the house," I said. "And I bet dads missed their families."

"Yes, I imagine many felt that way," she replied.

Mom went back to the computer and found several commercials highlighting suburban life. Tomorrow, we head home for a few weeks before our next road trip. ★

Today, we traveled to another small town. When my mom began planning her exhibit, she put an ad in local newspapers across the state. She was looking for anyone who would donate or lend artifacts of the time period to the museum. She received a call from a man who grew up during the Cold War and had saved many of his childhood mementos. We went to his town to look through his box of memories.

A War without Fighting

As we drove, my mom explained, "The artifacts we will look at today are related to the Cold War. The Cold War was not like a typical war. Its opponents did not have physical fighting or battles."

"Wait," I interrupted. "How can there be a war without battles?"

"A war with battles is a hot war. One without actual fighting is a cold war. The Cold War was mostly fear of what other countries would do," she said. "In World War II, the United States and the Soviet Union, which no longer exists, were on the same side. After the war, differing political policies and fear of each other's nuclear weapons led to the Cold War."

Before I could ask more, we arrived at our destination. A tall, thin man greeted us. He led us into his living room. There, he showed us four boxes.

"I kept a lot of my own things," he told us, "but I also collected items from friends and family." His wife brought us lemonade, and my mom put me to work sifting through the boxes with her. She told me to show her anything I found interesting.

Communism

My box contained mostly newspaper clippings. Many of them talked about communism or mentioned something called the red threat. I asked my mom what these were.

"Communism is a political system where the government controls the money and resources of a country," she said. "The U.S. economy is based on **capitalism**, which is when citizens and companies own the resources and they buy and sell them through a free market."

"But why is communism called the red threat?" I asked.

"The Soviet Union's army was called the Red Army, so communism became associated with the color red," our host jumped in. "The color red has symbolized revolution in Russia for many centuries."

Preparing for the Worst

Among the newspaper articles in my box, I found a journal entry. As I read it aloud, the man began to laugh:

Duck and cover drills are my favorite part of the day. Instead of having to do my math assignment, I huddle under my desk. We are supposed to cover our eyes and keep our necks and heads safely under the desks. But I usually trade baseball cards with my friends. Ms. Amara keeps reminding us that the threat of a nuclear attack is real, but it is hard to think of that when my friend has the baseball card I want. Last night, my dad talked about building an underground bomb shelter in our backyard, but I doubt he will get around to it.

Students participated in a duck and cover drill in the 1950s. This was a common practice at the time.

END OF THE COLD WAR

By the 1980s, many countries decided they wanted to end their experiment with communism and try democracy. This was also the case in the Soviet Union. The Soviet Union's end may give the impression that the United States won the Cold War. But not everyone agrees on the matter. Robert Gates, a former CIA director, asked, "Did we win or did the Soviets just lose?"

"I remember writing that in fifth grade," he said. "We practiced duck and cover drills, though they would have been useless in a real attack." He chuckled. "Follow me. I have something to show you."

We went into his backyard where he lifted a small cement hatch. We peered in with a flashlight. He explained that his dad began their shelter but never finished more than a four-foot hole in the ground. Inside the dark hole was a short ladder and the beginnings of a concrete wall on one side.

"My dad was never good at finishing things," our host explained.

We went back inside and finished our lemonade while he told us about some of his Cold War experiences. Although the United States was never attacked by the Soviet Union, people continued to live in fear of communism through the fall of the Soviet Union in 1991. My mom collected some artifacts, including the journal entry, before we made the long car trip home. ★

Today, we reached the National Baseball Hall of Fame and Museum in Cooperstown, New York. My mom wants to include some sports memorabilia in her exhibit. We took a guided tour arranged specially for us by a curator to help my mom choose artifacts. The tour guide told us the story of Jackie Robinson, the first African American baseball player in the major league. I thought his story was the most interesting I had heard on these trips with my mom.

The Negro National League

Before 1947, African American baseball players were not allowed to play on major league teams. They played in the Negro National League, which had only African Americans. Their teams were kept separate from the teams of white players.

The Pittsburgh Crawfords were the 1935 Negro National League Champions.

Breaking Barriers

As we looked at his uniform on display, the tour guide told us about the Brooklyn Dodgers' president, Branch Rickey.

"He was determined," she said, "to bring an African American into the major league. He saw something special in Jackie Robinson. In 1947, Robinson made his debut with the Dodgers." As she spoke, I stared at his Dodgers uniform. His glove was also on display.

"That glove," the tour guide said when she noticed me staring at it, "helped Robinson to become the first player to win Rookie of the Year, which happened in 1947, and Most Valuable Player in 1949. Despite his success, Robinson faced racial insults from fans and fellow players his entire career. Rickey chose Robinson to break the color barrier because he thought Robinson had the strength to handle the situation well, and Rickey was right. Robinson battled racism the rest of his life. He had successfully created a path for African Americans into professional sports, but they still faced a long road to full acceptance."

The tour guide walked to the next case, but I wasn't ready to move on. "Can you tell me more about Robinson?" I asked.

She walked back to his exhibit. "After leaving the league in 1957, he spent the rest of his life in business and civil rights **activism**," she explained. "He started several businesses aimed at helping African Americans succeed. He became a role model in the civil rights movement, which fought for racial equality, including ending the racial segregation that was so firmly rooted in the South."

The Civil Rights Movement

The tour guide explained that World War II and the Cold War fueled the civil rights movement. "Many Americans were horrified

Jackie Robinson's talent as a baseball player garnered
him awards and helped him become a civil rights leader.

15

by how the Nazis treated the Jews during World War II. Some began to rethink their own racism," she said. "Then, during the Cold War, the Soviets argued that the United States couldn't be a great country because of the prejudice there. Civil rights gained momentum in the 1940s and 1950s since Americans wanted to be the best country in the world. The nation was willing to improve its faults, especially in the area of racism," the guide said.

"But it was the actions of people such as Robinson that really made a difference," she said. "He even made appearances with Martin Luther King Jr., the leader of the civil rights movement."

"Wow, he was so much more than a baseball player!" I exclaimed.

"Yes," she said. "In 1962, Robinson became the first African American inducted into the Baseball Hall of Fame. Major league baseball retired his number, 42, from the entire league in April 1997, the fiftieth anniversary of his breaking the color barrier. In 2004, the league declared April 15 Jackie Robinson Day. Since 2009, on that day, the players, coaches, and umpires wear the number 42 to honor Jackie Robinson's **legacy**."

I learned more about the history of baseball during our tour. The courage of Jackie Robinson has really stayed with me. I will not forget what I learned today. ★

AN INSPIRATION

The success of the civil rights movement has inspired other groups to seek equality. Its practice of nonviolent changes has prompted similar activities by groups seeking their own advances. These groups include women, Chicanos, American Indians, and gays.

Today, we drove to an estate sale. My mom learned about the sale in the newspaper and saw it would include artifacts from the Vietnam War. As we drove to the sale, she told me the war began in 1957 and did not end until 1975.

Trying to Stop the Spread of Communism

She gave me more background information to help me understand the war. "The Vietnam War was fought as part of the

A U.S. soldier hurried from a thatched house
in South Vietnam after setting fire to it.

U.S. helicopters and troops in Vietnam during the war there.

larger Cold War between the United States and the Soviet Union, though the two powers didn't fight directly. North Vietnam was communist. South Vietnam was not. North Vietnam wanted to reunite North and South Vietnam under communism. The United States went to Vietnam to keep that from happening in an attempt to stop the spread of communism."

We arrived at the sale and found the item my mom was interested in: a U.S. soldier's uniform. It even included a medal of honor. My mom eagerly bought the uniform. I looked carefully at the medal, imagining what the soldier may have done to deserve it.

My Lai

I reached into one of the uniform's pockets and found a folded, worn paper. It was a newspaper article from 1969 about the My Lai **massacre**. I showed it to my mom, and she immediately went to find some of the family who had attended the estate sale. I quickly followed her. Mom asked several people if they knew why the soldier had kept the newspaper article in his pocket, but no one knew. Finally, an old woman with bright blue eyes approached my mother.

"He kept it as a reminder," the woman explained. She was the man's neighbor. She said, "It was a reminder that any person can do things in war they never imagined they would do. He wanted to remember to be the same kind of person he was back home."

"Thank you for your explanation," my mom said. We walked back to the uniform, and she let me read the article as she continued to look at the details of the uniform. The article explained that on March 16, 1968, a group of U.S. soldiers entered the village of My Lai to look for members of the North Vietnam army. The war in Vietnam was difficult because the members of that army did not wear uniforms. This made it very hard to identify if a person was a civilian or soldier.

When the U.S. soldiers arrived at the village, they did not find any army members there. Still, the man in charge, Lieutenant William Calley Jr., told his troops to gather the villagers in a group. Calley told his soldiers they knew what to do, so the soldiers guarded the villagers. Calley came back and told his soldiers to kill the villagers. The soldiers shot the villagers, including old men, women, and children—approximately 300 people.

The U.S. army tried to keep the massacre a secret, but it was revealed to the public in 1969. Americans were shocked that the soldiers would willingly kill so many civilians. As I finished the article, I understood why the soldier would keep it in the pocket of his uniform. He wanted to remember that under difficult circumstances, he might do something that terrible and regret it the rest of his life.

WAR TACTICS

Guerrilla warfare is the term used to describe the type of combat used by the North Vietnamese against U.S. troops during the Vietnam War. It's a tactic in which a smaller army ambushes a larger force. In Vietnam, the North Vietnamese soldiers dressed in civilian clothing to confuse the Americans fighting there. The North Vietnamese also had an extensive system of underground tunnels. These tactics had U.S. soldiers constantly on the lookout for the enemy in unexpected places.

Americans Respond to the War

On the way home, my mom told me the Vietnam War divided Americans between those who supported the war and those who protested against it.

"It was a war that could not be won," she said quietly. "And in 1975, the United States retreated from the country completely, allowing Vietnam to be fully under communist rule. However, it is not as strictly communist as other communist nations. Small businesses are thriving and people have a relatively decent standard of living."

"And Americans visit Vietnam all the time," I said. "Aunt Sally talked about the delicious food she ate on her vacation there."

"That's right," my mom agreed. "For a while, the United States would not trade with Vietnam. But today, the countries are friendlier with one another. People in both countries benefit from trading and visiting with each other." ★

This afternoon, my mom came home with a guitar case. I thought it was a gift for me, but it was another item for her exhibit. She opened the case to show me a beaten-up acoustic guitar. It was covered in stickers of flowers and peace symbols and had several autographs. She pointed out Bob Dylan's autograph and suggested I find out who he was.

Music and Drugs

I searched our local library's Web site for information about Dylan. I discovered he is an important folk rock artist who started writing songs in the 1960s. Singers of this generation wanted to end war and have more love and peace. They tried to create a new way of life that involved no war, only love and community. This new way of life was called a counterculture, and many of these people were often called hippies.

BABY BOOMERS

The young people who became known as hippies were part of the baby boom generation. This group of Americans, known simply as baby boomers, was born after World War II, from 1946 to 1964. Baby boomers have influenced everything from education to housing to health care to senior living.

This aerial photograph shows the massive crowd at Woodstock in 1969.

I looked up other artists who autographed the guitar, including Jimi Hendrix, Ringo Starr from the Beatles, and Keith Richards of the Rolling Stones, I noticed that articles about the musicians usually said something about drugs. I found that many musicians of the time talked about drugs in their songs.

"Why did all of these rock-and-roll stars talk about drugs?" I asked my mom.

She hesitated a minute and then explained. "In the 1960s, drugs became popular. However, people didn't know or care about the harmful effects drugs had on their body and minds. We can look back and see the negative effects. People still do drugs today, but as a society, we know drugs can cause serious health and personal problems."

Woodstock

Another signature on the guitar was from Janis Joplin. When I looked up her name, I found out about Woodstock, a music festival that many hippies and college students attended. Woodstock took place on a farm in Bethel, New York, in August 1969. The festival was organized for approximately 50,000 people, but 500,000 came. There was not enough water, food, or bathrooms for the crowds. The people who attended helped each other live through the lack of supplies and space to enjoy songs popular at the time. Some songs protested the Vietnam War and upheld the civil rights cause.

Hippies

Many people who attended Woodstock became hippies—some even lived in communes. These groups of people wanted to go back to the basics of living off the land without using consumer products. The people in these communes shared all of their resources, including money, and they said they were all one family.

After what I learned about the horrors of the My Lai massacre, it was easy for me to understand why the counterculture developed. People saw the problems with the Vietnam War and were angry about the unequal treatment of people. So, they rejected U.S. culture. Many focused on using drugs and not taking part in mainstream society. ★

This photograph shows two of the 500,000 people who attended Woodstock in 1969. This couple is an example of hippies.

MISSION ACCOMPLISHED!

You did it! You now understand the atmosphere of the time in U.S. history following World War II through the early 1970s. You know about the economic boom that followed the war. You learned about the impact the Cold War and the Vietnam War had on Americans. The Cold War created an atmosphere of fear where average Americans practiced duck and cover drills and created shelters in their backyards to protect themselves in the event of a nuclear attack. The Vietnam War's bloody fighting contrasted the hippie culture. You also discovered the role Jackie Robinson played in the civil rights movement during and after his baseball career. Good job!

CONSIDER THIS

★ If you lived in the 1950s, would you choose to live in the city or the suburbs? Why?

★ The Vietnam War is famous for dividing Americans. Name another recent event that divided the nation and explain why people disagreed.

★ Many singers and bands in the 1960s wrote music that went against the major culture of the United States at that time. What types of music written today go against the culture?

You can visit the Vietnam Veterans Memorial in Washington, DC, and see this statue. It honors the soldiers who fought in the war.

GLOSSARY

activism (AK-tiv-iz-uhm) actions taken to change a political idea in a nation

archive (AHR-kive) a place where historical documents are stored safely

capitalism (KAP-i-tuh-liz-uhm) a system of making money for personal gain

communism (KAHM-yuh-niz-uhm) a system where money is controlled by the community or government, not individuals

counterculture (KOUN-tur-KUHL-chur) a lifestyle of people, usually young, who reject the values and lifestyle that dominate their country

curator (KYOOR-ay-tur) the person who chooses and organizes the items in museum displays

domestic (duh-MES-tik) related to the home

exhibit (ig-ZIB-it) a collection of objects placed in a public area for people to see

hippie (HIP-ee) a young person in the 1960s who rejected the established culture and promoted peace and love

legacy (LEG-uh-see) a gift handed down to the next generation

massacre (MAS-uh-kur) the unnecessary killing of a number of human beings

suburb (SUHB-urb) a residential area close to but outside a city

BOOKS

Gourley, Catherine. *Gidgets and Women Warriors: Perceptions of Women in the 1950s and 1960s.* Brookfield, CT: Twenty First Century Books, 2007.

Hill, Laban Carrick. *America Dreaming: How Youth Changed America in the Sixties.* New York, NY: Little, Brown, 2007.

Markovitz, Hal. *The Vietnam War.* Detroit, MI: Lucent Books, 2007.

Teitelbaum, Michael. *Jackie Robinson: Champion for Equality.* New York, NY: Sterling, 2010.

WEB SITES

The Cold War Museum
http://www.coldwar.org

Explore timelines and test your knowledge with a Cold War trivia game.

Guess the Year
http://pbskids.org/historydetectives/games/60stimecapsule/index2.html

Take on the detective mission to identify the year using clues at this PBS site.

MISSION 1

Although the Cold War is over, the possibility of nuclear war still exists. Research what countries are developing or have nuclear weapons. What has the United States done to lessen the threat of nuclear attack? What positive ways is nuclear energy being used?

MISSION 2

Because of Jackie Robinson's courage and determination, there are many African Americans in professional sports today. Research your favorite African American athlete. What was the athlete's childhood like? What path did he or she take to become a professional athlete? Who helped the athlete achieve success? What do you admire about the athlete?

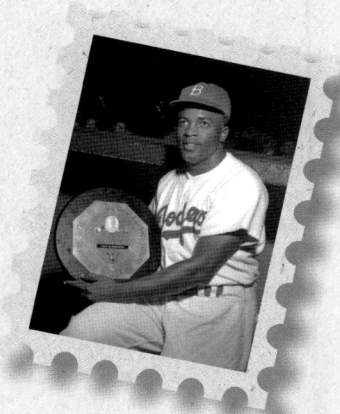

ABOUT THE AUTHOR

Maggie Combs taught middle school language arts. She is now a freelance writer and office manager. She lives in Minnesota with her husband and cat.

ABOUT THE CONSULTANTS

Michelle Kuhl grew up in North Carolina, went to upstate New York for her history PhD, taught in Texas for two years, and currently works at the University of Wisconsin Oshkosh. She has two daughters: one who thinks she is a fairy princess, and one who thinks she is a descendent of a Greek god. Both of them like going to the library with their mortal mom.

Gail Saunders-Smith is a former classroom teacher and Reading Recovery teacher leader. Currently, she teaches literacy courses at Youngstown State University in Ohio. Gail is the author of many books for children and three professional books for teachers.